MW01602054

Unlocking Your 20/20 Vision

Angel Michelle Chapman-McDavid, JD

Copyright © 2024 Angel Michelle Chapman-McDavid, JD

All rights reserved.

ISBN: 9798651961061

Dedication

Unlocking Your 20/20 Vision is dedicated first to my 17 grandchildren (Juwan, Jasmyn, RJ, RaeYonna, Johnathan, Chase, Mya, Maria, Mark, Noah, Karlie (rest in peace), Braylon, RJ Jr., Nolan, Juwan Jr., Riley, Karlee, and Ahrian). I may not be able to see you all on a regular basis but know that I love each and every one of you.

Secondly, I want to thank my parents, Sheila & Dale Kelly; my maternal grandparents, Dorothy & Norman Roscoe and my paternal grandparents, Ruth & Percy Kelly for sharing their love and concern for me, while showing me how to be a loving mother and grandmother to my children and grandchildren. Thank you, Papa Ted, for being an extra special one of my acquired parental units and showing up whenever it really counts!

Thirdly, I must express my undying love for all my children, as you have made me so proud. I am amazed that you all survived and thrived, despite my imperfections as a mother. I thank you for the blessing of being your mom, and I want you to know that you all, in your own special individual ways, hold a very special place in my heart. I know you've been through a lot with me, some good and some not so good, but know that I never ever stopped loving you, no matter the circumstances. I loved you before you officially came into my life, and I will love you for all eternity. God made each one of you just for me!

Last, but certainly not least, I dedicate this book to my late stepdaughter, Brittany. I wish I had had an opportunity to get to know you, as I know we would have gotten along famously. I have heard so many good things about you from your dad, and through my love for him, I have grown to love you and your son. Know that I am taking good care of your dad and that I will always love him to the ends of the earth. Rest in peace, Sweetheart…

Table of Contents

Chapter 1 – The Early Years

Chapter 2 – Growing Up

Chapter 3 - Teenagers Are from Mars

Chapter 4 – Becoming A Young Adult

Chapter 5 – Life Starts to Get Real

Chapter 6 – The Struggle

Chapter 7 – There is a God

Chapter 8 – It's Gets Worse Before It Gets Better

Chapter 9 – Dreams Do Come True

Chapter 10 – Can't Wait to See What's Next

The Preface

Guess What? The 111-day countdown to the bar exam ends today. It ends because I do not have to be a superwoman. I can put my cape in the closet, as my sponsor, Alesia, used to tell me. I have decided to make the decision to walk in my success, being determined by ME; and I decided the bar exam can wait until I am ready to sufficiently prepare for such an all-encompassing exam, without a million other things on my plate, spilling over and trying to make a figurative mess (in my head) ... or not.

My Father is pleased with my progress in life; my friends and family members look up to and admire me; and I have made my mama proud (according to her, that happened long before now). I can simply live my life, putting one foot in front of the other, doing the next right thing, for the right reasons, and all will be well. Besides, my mom gave me permission to be a full-fledged adult and make whatever decisions I need to make for myself, and she will be pleased and supportive.

Thanks Mom...Shall we call this chapter three...The fall season...Take one? Maybe we will just keep it 100 and call it *Unlocking Your 20/20 Vision*...

My Ten Guiding Principles

1. **Love** – I am committed to loving out loud, with care, concern, and intention – including myself.

2. **Freedom** – I am committed to being an advocate and an ally for freedom, on every level and for everyone.

3. **Diversity** – I am committed to respecting, and appreciating, the rights, choices, lifestyles, and unique cultures of all mankind.

4. **Success** – I am committed to living my best life, personally and professionally, while making a positive impact on my small corner of the world, and beyond.

5. **Spirituality** – I am committed to remain strong in my faith, in close dependence upon, and in communion with, God.

6. **Security** – I am committed to protecting myself, and my loved ones, from all hurt, harm, and danger, to the best of my ability – of course, remembering that I must first take care of myself before I can effectively help others.

7. **Joy** – I am committed to maintaining a consistent level of joy in my heart, despite the circumstances or challenges of life and the world.

8. **Peace** – I am committed to living a peaceful and serene life filled with opportunities to grow and share with others.

9. **Integrity** – I am committed to operating in a perpetual state of honesty, first to myself, then to others – even when nobody's looking.

10. **Authenticity** – I am committed to being the best version of me possible.

9 Facts About Me That Make Me Who I AM...

1. ...Raised by a super, hard-working single mom, with very high standards and expectations for herself, and me...because I was her whole world (and I still am...well almost).

2. ...Lived a life of privilege, as a little brown girl, in a world-renown, beautiful, resource-filled, predominantly white, suburban community known for diversity, excellent schools, amazing opportunities, and expectations of success.

3. ...Received an amazing private and public-school education, showing promise, talent, and ambition, before entering college at age 17, and beginning a journey that would begin to shape the trajectory of my life.

4. ...At the risk of becoming a statistic, I started my family at the age of 19; and began what would become my identity, the most important aspect and greatest accomplishment of my life...it all happened just a little too soon. I became a mom.

5. ...Being the hopeless romantic, with traditional family values, ideals, and typical little girl dreams, I sought to correct my lack of order, as it pertained to my major young adult life decisions, and I got married; I had more children; grew up and grew into maturity and motherhood, loving every minute of it. Then I got divorced...tried to fix the mistakes made in many young marriages, by getting up and dusting myself off, and trying again...and again...and again...but now I am not young anymore.

6. The challenges and uncertainties of life led me down the path of alcoholism, as I struggled to cope with what felt like failures, on so many levels of my life. I thought I would never escape the deep, dark hole of despair....... Until I did.

7. ...On July 1, 2003, God saved me from me. He blessed me with the gift of sobriety and opened the doors to a whole new life. He has allowed me to live two lives in one. By His Grace and Mercy, I have awakened with sober eyes for more than 21 years, through all the good; all the bad; all the sunshine; all the rain: and through it all, God has been with me as I walked through all the storms, with grace. My sobriety has not only withstood the test of time, but it has also courageously faced breast cancer, divorce, the loss of loved ones, and endured the pain of my children and grandchildren, at various times, being affected by serious illness, addiction, trauma, and violent crime that could have taken their lives...and by God's Grace, I didn't drink... and they are all still here.

8. ...That gift of sobriety, along with the love and support of my friends and family, afforded me the opportunity to accomplish some goals and realize some dreams (and make my mama, daddy, and children proud):
    a. I completed my undergraduate degree 33 years after graduating high school (and I graduated at the top of my class).
    b. I completed my law degree 3 years later.
    c. I have owned and operated a small business for over 21 years.
    d. I am a nonprofit leader in my community.

      e. I have only 5-6 classes left to complete my master's degree, in Human Resource Management (I should probably do that).

      f. In the year 2020, I published my first book and started writing my second book – the one you are reading now!

9. ...Sometimes it's okay to start over; Because without a test, there is no testimony! My liabilities can now be used as assets, and potentially impact someone else, to the degree of changing their life's trajectory. Perhaps, the next life I will have the privilege of positively affecting is yours! Let us ride this train of Unlocking Your 20/20 Vision together!

...This is my story. First, and foremost, I am an imperfect child of God. Second, I am a survivor. Third, my name is Angel, and I am a grateful recovered alcoholic, **and so much more**! Praise be to God!

Chapter 1 – The Early Years

In the 1461 days it takes to complete an undergraduate college degree, I experienced every emotion known to mankind and discovered the formula to acquire the insight needed to move on and close that chapter of my life; but it didn't all start there. The story of unlocking my 20/20 vision started 19,079 days before the day that would forever change my life and the life of my entire family. May 26, 2016, felt like the scariest of nightmares, the one from which you long to wake up, but simply cannot.

This journey of unlocking my 20/20 vision is very much predicated on my own perception of events and circumstances that have occurred throughout my life. Respectfully, I acknowledge my perception, and perspective, to perhaps be different from that of others, namely my children and parents.

According to the Merriam-Webster dictionary, the definition of ***perception*** is an awareness of the elements of environment through physical sensation interpreted in the light of experience; a quick, acute, and intuitive cognition; a capacity for comprehension. The definition of ***perspective*** is a mental view or prospect; a visible scene; the interrelation in which a subject or its parts are mentally viewed; the capacity to view things in their true relations or relative importance.

My view, though not necessarily the one that matters most, is the perspective from which this story will be told, as it is the one with which I am most intimately familiar, and by which I (and those around me) am most directly affected. Fortunately, or unfortunately, I have very little memory of life before first grade, as the stories I've been told by my parents and grandparents involved some traumatic events, as it pertains to my family dynamics. My parents married young, had me, endured the natural (and not so natural) challenges of marriage before divorcing in a few short years. Their separation caused my mom and me to move to Boston, Massachusetts shortly after the Boston Strangler confessed to murdering 13 women in the Greater Boston area. Perhaps we could have moved elsewhere?

We remained in Boston for a relatively short period of time, as my maternal grandmother (Nanny) faked a heart condition to get my mother to return home to Cleveland, Ohio. The ploy worked; we returned home to my grandparents, and mom began her career in the real estate industry. By this time, I was ready to start Kindergarten at Moreland Elementary School before transferring to Holy Family, a Catholic School, for first grade. The reason I remember first grade is because I got into a fight with a child 3 years older than me (she had failed first grade twice) and got beat up over a pencil; one that she accused me of stealing from her. That was traumatic for me, as it sent me across the street to my mother's real estate office bleeding, bruised, and terrified. By the way, I did not steal that girl's pencil!

That physical altercation was all it took for mom to purchase a lovely two-family Tudor-style home in Shaker Heights, a racially integrated, yet predominantly white suburb on the east side of Cleveland, transfer me to St. Dominic's School for second grade (the Catholic School in Shaker Heights), and enroll me in gymnastics, ballet, and modern dance classes. This was the beginning of what would become my life – full of experiences, exposure, and opportunities for future success (with very little down time).

To say we were busy would be an understatement. Mom worked on average of 75 hours per week, while I did school, homework, extra-curricular activities, some weekends with my dad, Sunday dinners, and most weekends at my grandparents. It was a great childhood, one where all my needs were met and most of my desires were fulfilled. I had begun to live a life of privilege, as a little brown girl in a world-renowned, predominantly white, suburban community known for diversity, excellent schools, amazing opportunities, and expectations for success. All of which I neither understood nor appreciated.

Chapter 2 – Growing Up

Being an only child certainly has its ups and downs. Yes, I was spoiled and got just about everything I wanted, but it was an incredibly lonely existence. I longed for siblings. I wanted desperately to have someone with which to share a room, the television, or the telephone. I wanted someone to fight with, someone to blame when things went wrong; I wanted a sister or a brother to hang out with and ultimately help raise. But none of that was happening, at least not if I was depending upon my mother to make it happen. She was more than content with her only child. I was her entire world, and I still am (almost).

My father, on the other hand, saw things a bit differently. I am the oldest of his four biological children, one of which I didn't meet until August 4, 2019 – thanks for the beautiful dinner meeting, Mom! That sibling is my sister, Joy, who is 2 years, 2 months, and 22 days younger than me (2222 is my favorite number for several reasons that you will understand later). That story is enough for a whole book in itself! Just suffice it to say that it was a huge blessing to meet, get to know, and love her. Joy and I have a very special relationship that I'm sure will be in place for a lifetime, as she is a beautiful human being inside and out.

My dad believed in the try, try again method (that must be where I got it). Within a few years of my parents' divorce, Dad remarried and gave me the brother I always wanted. It didn't happen quite the way I had envisioned, but it was a close second. We didn't grow up in the same household, but Todd was a sweetheart of a child. I loved him and my mother loved him, as well. I got to spend time with him when I had weekends with my dad, and he occasionally spent time with me and my mom. Unfortunately, Todd had a very serious accident when he was two years old. He fell down the stairs causing him to have a traumatic brain injury that left him permanently disabled and suffering throughout his short 40-year life.

I miss my brother. I wish he had more time to spend with me and the family, but I am grateful for having the opportunity to know and love him. I am proud of him for the accomplishments he was able to attain, despite his disability. He graduated from high school, was an avid weightlifter, and had an amazing sense of humor. A close friend of mine once told me that people come into our lives for a reason, a season, or a lifetime, and I believe Todd is one of the people God brought into my life for a short season – a season to learn patience, unconditional love, and how to appreciate the differences and disabilities of others.

That marriage didn't work out for my dad, so he picked himself up, dusted himself off, and tried again. Unfortunately, that one didn't work out either, but I did gain a wonderful stepbrother, Matthew, out of the deal; and he has been a part of my life, somewhat from a distance, ever since. I think Matt is one of the people meant to be in my life for a lifetime.

In an effort to get it right, Dad married again and this time it worked! He married Laverne, who would be the mother of my youngest sister, Pat. Shortly after they married, they moved from Cleveland, Ohio to Greensboro, North Carolina, and my sister was born shortly thereafter. So, once again, I have another sibling that I did not grow up with; but of course, I love her dearly.

Another person I believe came into my life for a lifetime is my very close friend named Shelli, who would be the first of a group of friends called the Beeches (you can use your imagination). Shelli and I lived across the street from one another, and her parents were so cool! We went shopping, skiing, bowling, and out to eat together, all the time. Occasionally, Shelli and I found ourselves in a little hot water, but for the most part, we were pretty good kids. Our Moms were friends too, so it made for a very fulfilling and fun friendship. I was a latchkey kid, so whenever I would lose my house keys, I would go to Shelli's house and wait for my mom to come home. Eventually, Mom decided to give her mom keys to our house, since it was evident that I would continue misplacing my keys on a regular basis! Sorry Mom!

Mom was working a gazillion hours, I was the budding gymnast, doing cartwheels, flips, and splits all over the place, a stellar student, and spending most of my free time with my grandparents. I had an amazing relationship with Nanny and Grandpa – a child couldn't have asked for a better grandparent experience. They fed me well, spoiled me rotten (okay maybe not rotten), spent lots of quality time with me, and taught me what it meant to be a loving and caring grandparent. My grandfather even taught me how to drive when I was 12, without Nanny's knowledge of course. By the time she found out, I was backing out of the driveway and well on my way to being a competent, experienced driver! That got Grandpa in a world of trouble with Nanny and Mom, but it was too late. I already knew how to drive! Thanks Grandpa!

By this time, I was just about ready to graduate from junior high school and move on to high school. My mother, being highly protective and having very little faith in public schools, gave me the option of attending Glen Oak School for Girls or Villa Maria Academy High School in Pennsylvania. Since I didn't want to get shipped off to boarding school, I chose Glen Oak, which was only 30 minutes from my house.

Upon attending the Open House for Glen Oak, I met Darlene, who would become my best friend. She definitely falls within the lifetime category, as she is still my best friend today. We grew up together, we got in trouble together, we laughed together, we cried together, eventually we lived together, and so much more! There are only a handful of people to which I can say, "I owe you my life," and she is definitely one of them. I love you, Darlene…always…

Chapter 3 – Teenagers are From Mars

Glen Oak School for Girls was an amazing, supportive, and experiential learning journey for all who were in attendance. The students received a world-class education in a quiet, non-traditional, open classroom setting, with comfortable couches, loveseats, and recliners, in place of hard desks and chairs. The student teacher ratio was about 9:1 on average, except for math classes that were taught in a more traditional classroom setting.

Glen Oak was the definition of privilege. We wore a wide variety of attractive yet practical uniforms (so we wouldn't get bored); we received individual instruction, when necessary; and our field trips took place all over the world. The school administrators and educators were intentionally concerned with our learning experience, from a holistic perspective that included academic excellence, mental and emotional health, self-esteem, and our general well-being. The Glen Oak experience was just that, a journey that helped shape the trajectory of the rest of my life – good, bad, and indifferent, but mostly good.

As a teenager I found life very difficult. I was sheltered and growing into young womanhood, with raging hormones, the body of a twenty-year old, and a mindset that told me I could accomplish anything, if only I was good enough. Despite all the internal and external positive reinforcement, I never quite felt deserving of success. I thought I could never really live up to the expectations of my mother who taught me that I could be anything I wanted to be, if I was willing to do the work. She kept me on that only child pedestal that oftentimes made me feel like a failure when I made a mistake. And, trust me, I made many! Today I know and understand that she did her best and gave her all for my wellbeing and future success. Too bad kids don't come with an instruction manual, right?

My teenage years were challenging, yet I still managed to do well academically. I know it was a tumultuous time for my mother, as well, as she was doing everything in her power to raise me right, expose me to the finer things in life, and provide me with every opportunity for success. Mom was loving and affectionate and perhaps a bit overprotective, as were the other members of my family, including my dad, my uncles, and grandparents. I really couldn't have asked for more (except maybe to have been allowed to cross the street without permission at 15 years old). I was given almost anything I wanted, but I just didn't know what I didn't know. Most everything was taken for granted, as I felt entitled to much more than I was given, and I just couldn't understand why I couldn't have the fairytale life I had dreamed of.

I wanted two parents who lived in the same house, a brother, a sister, a bigger house (okay, I wanted to live in a mansion like some of my friends), a dog, a housekeeper (oh yeah, we had a housekeeper), my own car, and I wanted to be trusted to live without rules and chores. If only mom had allowed me to live that life, everything would have been okay, right?

Well, it didn't quite work out that way. Instead, I lived a life that sent me to private school, attended overnight summer camp for ten summers in a row (I had to beg to get a job at 15 years old), went to New York City and Detroit for shopping excursions, vacationed in Florida and New York, attended musicals, plays, concerts, sporting events, and even saw *Hair* on Broadway. I was traumatized during the scene when they all appeared on stage naked! Mom wasn't expecting that! I truly lived a life of privilege and didn't even know it, because it was normal. Thank you for a wonderful childhood, Mom.

One of the reasons my mother had no faith in public education was because of all the alcohol and drugs that seemed to be prevalent in the schools, especially at the high school level. She felt I would be better off in a more exclusive environment where parents paid for their children's education, and she wanted to expose me to a life and opportunities that I might otherwise have missed in the public-school environment. Unfortunately, what she didn't realize was the effect of kids having more access to money, and less supervision as it pertained to obtaining drugs and alcohol, and how that might affect me. She just didn't know what she didn't know. Her efforts to protect me from an inferior education, a mediocre mentality, and random acts of crime was successful; but her attempt to shield me from drugs and alcohol were not.

Every year, during the month of May, Glen Oak students would sign up to go away somewhere in the country (or the world) for a week, as an extended field trip. For my freshman year I decided to go to West Virginia because my best friend, Darlene, was going, and because Mrs. D, our biology teacher, was the chaperone. Mrs. D was the coolest teacher in the school, so we figured we would have a good time. So off we go on the chartered bus to West Virginia, laughing, talking, and having a good ole time. When we arrived at our motel, Mrs. D told us to meet her in her room at 9:00pm sharp because she had a surprise for us. The fifteen of us were super excited because we thought we were going to have a pizza party or something!

When we arrived at Mrs. D's room, she had us all huddled around the bathroom door, in anticipation, and then she opened the door to reveal a bathtub full of ice, beer, wine, and other types of alcohol! We were shocked! We could hardly believe that our teacher and chaperone had bought us alcoholic beverages and some illegal drugs for the trip! That was my first introduction to drugs and alcohol at 15 years of age. I know you're wondering whether I indulged in the drinking, and all, and the answer is a resounding YES! I was an impressionable teenager who was surrounded by other obviously happy kids who were drinking, smoking, snorting, sniffing, and more – what's the saying? When in Rome, do as the Romans?

I found myself drunk and hungover the entire trip. I even called my mother, while inebriated, and laughed and giggled on the phone. What else was I to do? I did not know what you were supposed to do when you got drunk! Of course, we were all sworn to secrecy about the events of Mini-Week in West Virginia, but the secret is out now (oops). In the meantime, we returned home to Cleveland, Ohio, kept our mouths shut, enjoyed summer vacation, went back to school, and waited for the next Mini-Week.

It was sophomore year and time for Mini-Week. This time I chose to go to Wyoming because I heard it was a beautiful part of the country, Darlene was going, and Mrs. D was the chaperone. You already know the rest of the story!

Despite the debacle of Wyoming and West Virginia, I managed to keep my head on straight enough to continue doing well in school, drinking only on occasion, and only running away from home from time to time. I was driving my mother insane! I was a super-moody teenager from Mars who had to see a therapist on a weekly basis, as I was struggling with depression, crazy emotional highs, and lows, talking too fast, not sleeping enough, and never feeling I was good enough. After a few suicide attempts and hospitalizations, my mother took the advice of an emergency room doctor to have me psychiatrically evaluated. That evaluation produced a diagnosis of bi-polar disorder, which explained the highs and lows, suicidal ideation, grandiosity, and general low self-esteem. Mom then realized I wasn't just a moody teenager, I was sick and needed medication and continued therapy.

Being the loving and conscientious mother that she was, I received all of that and more. I was able to get stabilized, skip 11th grade, transfer to Shaker Heights High School (the public school), graduate, and go off to college at Ohio University in Athens, Ohio. I was 17 years old and academically prepared to tackle the next phase of my life. Whether I was socially and emotionally ready for college is up for debate, but I finally got to live my life the way I wanted to and become who I wanted to be. I thought I had arrived. I was finally an adult.

Chapter 4 – Becoming a Young Adult

College life at Ohio University – where do I begin? Perhaps I should start with my first quarter when I got invited to my first campus Harry Buffalo party. I quickly learned that Harry Buffalo consisted of 190 proof Grain Alcohol mixed with Hawaiian punch and lots of fruit. It was housed in large trash cans lined with black trash bags and tasted like sweet fruit punch, with a little kick to it. It was delicious! It was so delicious that I drank six or seven large red cups, blacked out, and then awakened in my room the next day, sick as a dog! I was terribly ill for the next several days, with fluids coming out of every orifice of my body. I thought I would die! I called home and told mom I had a bad case of the flu and thought I needed to go home; but she assured me I would be okay and to check back in over the weekend. I got better, but I now know that illness was a bad case of alcohol poisoning. That should have been my warning.

The second and third quarters were much like the first – go to class, party, sleep, party, study, party, and repeat. Those days of academic excellence were long gone. College was the real deal, and my drinking did not help matters. It didn't help that I was not taking my medication, except on occasion, because I felt great most of the time. I felt like I was in control and could manage the emotional highs and lows with a few drinks.

By the grace of God, I made it through my first year, went home for the summer, and returned to O.U. for fall quarter of my sophomore year. That went a little better, as I was beginning to learn the lay of the land and figure out what I needed to do to be somewhat successful, academically speaking. Grades improved, fall semester ended and I headed home for the much-needed six-week winter break. I spent lots of quality time with family and friends and enjoyed the Thanksgiving and Christmas holidays.

Shortly after returning to school the following January, I realized that I had a surprise baking in the oven – my oven – I was pregnant! Oh, my goodness, how did this happen? I guess I spent a little too much quality time with a certain young man that I had known from the neighborhood. I had just started my second year of college, and I didn't know what to do! All I knew was that I always wanted to be a mom. I had dreams and fantasies of motherhood, since I was about 12 years old, and often thought of all the things I would do with my baby, when I became a mother. Perhaps it was due to the extreme loneliness of growing up as an only child. I had begged my mom for siblings, and she always said that one of me was more than enough! This baby could be the answer to the unbearable loneliness that I had suffered. I would never again be lonely because I would have my own little mini-me to nurture, care for, and love. Quickly, the decision was made – I would stop drinking, have my baby, become a mom, get married, go to college, graduate, and become a successful woman who beat the odds! I would have my own little family.

But it didn't quite work out that way. I did, in fact, quit drinking and have my baby. I had a beautiful, healthy, bouncing baby girl and named her Kelly (actually, my mother named her). I temporarily dropped out of college, returned home to Cleveland, got a job, and took care of my little young family – as a single mom. This had not turned out to be the fairytale I had imagined, but the one saving grace was the little girl who loved me unconditionally and depended upon me, literally, for everything. I was in love! I finally understood how my mother felt about me, because that little girl became my whole reason for living.

Thank goodness I had the support of my family and some very close friends (*The Beeches* – Shelli, Stefanie, Simone, Erika, Twyla, and Lanita) who helped me transition into motherhood. We, individually and collectively, had some fun, exciting, and hair-raising experiences that we laugh about today, but most importantly, we have a special love for one another that has withstood the test of time and distance. The Beeches babysat Kelly (and her siblings that would come later); but it was always so much more than simple babysitting. Kelly and I became a part of their families, and we spent lots of quality time with each one of them. I am reminded of the many nights spent at the Shaker Shanty and A Touch of Italy together – lots of pizza, White Zinfandel, Peach Schnapps, and Long Island Iced Tea! The Beeches fall into that lifetime category, as well. I will always have a special love for the Beeches!

I stayed in Cleveland for 18 months before returning to Ohio University, only this time I went as a mom. I got a nanny for my daughter, lived in student family housing, and continued my academic studies. I was determined not to be a statistic, and a college drop out. I wanted to prove the naysayers wrong, make something of my life, and gain my mother's approval. Time moved on; I had matured a little, concentrated on my studies, and even found my way to a small Baptist Church in Athens, where many of the Black students attended regularly.

One Sunday morning, as I sat in church, the preacher was preaching, the choir was singing, and the spirit was moving when suddenly, my little girl yelled out, "Mommy, meet my friend Jim!" I was so embarrassed as I held her in my arms trying to quiet her. She was insistent that I meet her new friend; so, I turned around, quietly said hello, and apologized for her outburst. Jim was a polite, young, conservatively dressed young white guy whom I had never seen before. The service concluded and my daughter proceeded to continue her conversation with Jim, causing him to ask if he could walk us home. Being polite, I said yes, and that was the beginning of a torrid, collegiate love affair that was destined for happily ever after.

Over the next several months, despite our differences and the challenges associated with an interracial relationship, Jim and I fell deeply in love. He was a kind, considerate, and intelligent English major, in addition to being a musician who played the organ for his local church back home. Jim was highly spiritual and planned to become an Episcopal priest after graduation. We had discussed raising a family in the Episcopal Church, as he was sure to be an amazingly dedicated priest, husband, and father.

Jim had been adopted into a loving family from a very small town in Ohio and I was from the big city. We could not have been any more different, yet we were inseparable and immediately knew we were destined to spend the rest of our lives together.

In the winter of that year, Jim proposed; I said yes, and we started planning an intimate, private ceremony to be held at one of the campus chapels. He bought me a beautiful dress, and our wedding rings, in preparation for the big day that was only a few weeks away. I was so excited! I was so in love! I, literally, didn't believe it possible to love or be loved the way Jim and I loved one another. This would be perfect! My family would be complete, and our lives would be full.

Of course, we had to share the good news with our parents, so we started with a trip to Jim's hometown, where the three of us would spend the weekend. We had a wonderful visit with his parents and younger siblings; his mother looked after Kelly so I could go to the church to hear Jim play the organ for choir rehearsal; we shared several meals, and had a wonderful, yet relatively uneventful weekend (except for my baby girl hiding in the clothes dryer from his mom). Mind you, this was Jim's mother's first up close and personal experience with someone Black, so I'm sure it was quite an ordeal for her.

We returned to campus and a few days later reached out to my dad with the news. He was cautiously optimistic, and happy for us, but expressed some concern around the expediency of the nuptials. Then we called my mom. Her reaction was not as calm and understanding as my dad's reaction. She was deeply disturbed and concerned about the ramifications of an interracial marriage. Being a young, highly successful, Black real estate professional, she had many negative, racially motivated encounters that left her fearful, and a bit jaded, about the possibility of a successful and sustaining interracial relationship. Mom thought Jim was an intelligent and polite young man, but not marriage material for her daughter – mostly because he was white. She also expressed concern around us getting married so soon, as she believed our love was only a passing phase, and not true love. Mom made it clear that we did not have her approval, and she would not be present for our wedding. I was devastated!

Jim tried to comfort me and reassure me that all would be well, despite her disapproval. We believed our love would conquer all, and that time would heal all wounds. So, we let a few days pass and then called his parents to confirm their attendance. Surprisingly, after such a nice weekend visit, we were met with similar expressions of disappointment and disapproval. This left us both hurt and broken. We loved each other so much yet felt an obligation to our parents. What were we to do?

We prayed and talked; we cried and talked; we wrote down pros and cons; we considered pushing the wedding back a few months, even a year…we just did not know what to do, but we had to do something. So, after several more days, we mutually agreed to cancel the wedding, end our relationship, and go our separate ways, purely for the sake of our parents. Jim declared that he would never marry, if he could not be married to me, and instead he would become a Catholic priest (and take a lifetime vow of celibacy). We cried; we hugged; we kissed; and went our separate ways. It was the hardest thing I had ever experienced at the time, and it changed the trajectory of my life. I knew I would never know love like that again, as I believed it to be a once in a lifetime experience.

Chapter 5 – Life Starts to Get Real

Yep – it just got real. Heartache…Heartbreak…Parenthood…Life on Life's Terms at 21 years old. Where would I go from here? I tried to be like my dad and pick myself up, dust myself off, and move forward – so I transferred from Ohio University to Kent State University to continue the pursuit of my undergraduate degree. Unfortunately, due to my excessive drinking, depression, and lack of focus, my tenure as a KSU student was short-lived. I figured the problem was Kent State, so I moved back to Cleveland, got a job, slowed down my drinking, and tried to pick up the pieces of my life.

Fortunately, I had some help and support from family and friends, namely the Beeches, and my good friend James who worked at the local pizza parlor. We had been close friends since we were 15 years old and had many friends in common. Oftentimes we were accused of having a romantic relationship, when we were only platonic friends, but we didn't let that interfere with our friendship. Though he was not my daughter's biological father, James treated my little one as his own. He babysat, fed us, bought her clothes and toys, and most importantly, he spent quality time with us both. It didn't take long to realize that he cared for us, as if we were *his* family. By the time Kelly was three years old, we decided to start dating. We figured we were being accused of it, anyway, so why not give it a try!

Within a few short months, we found ourselves expecting a baby of our own, so we decided to "do it right," and get married a couple of months before the baby was due. We married in September of that year and William was born in November. I finally had a son and a daughter, and a little family of my own. Perhaps this would be my happily ever after? James was a hard-working husband, a loyal friend, and a wonderful father to both children. We had our challenges, like most young couples with the responsibility of little humans, but we worked through them to the best of our ability.

Our challenges were exacerbated due to William being a sickly child, which caused me to be forced to quit my job and, subsequently, we experienced financial difficulties, but somehow, we always managed to bounce back. James worked lots of hours managing the neighborhood pizza parlor, and I started my own business to help with the family finances. I owned and operated a virtual secretarial service from my home office, took care of the children, the house, and my husband. Life was starting to move right along when I discovered I was, once again, pregnant. My older daughter had just started school, my son was still in diapers, and we were in shock!

Baby Marissa graced us with her presence 20 months after her brother's arrival. She was a sweetheart and a blessing from God. I had always said it was easier to have two children, as opposed to one, because they were company for one another. But, going from two little ones to three little ones was a different story. My hands were beyond full and at times it was a little overwhelming. I would often ask myself, "Isn't this what you always wanted, a big family with lots of children running around?" Remember, I was the lonely, only child who begged for siblings. My children would not have that problem!

Being a family of five was fun, interesting, and challenging. There was never a dull moment. The children were growing up; I was growing my business; and James was spending increased time at work. By now, he had left the pizza parlor to become a General Manager at McDonald's. He worked long hours, had lots of responsibility, and came home only to sleep. We were quickly growing increasingly distant, as husband and wife, and our relationship seemed to regress to roommates, at best. I knew something was very wrong…and I was right.

James had begun having an extramarital affair, with one of his employees, that explained the excessive time away from home, the late nights, and the emotional distance between us. I confronted him about the situation and followed him to his mistress' apartment one night after work. As you can imagine that night did not end well, and it wasn't long thereafter that I packed up the children, our belongings, and moved out. My baby girl was only 11 months old at the time.

The separation was relatively civil, as we had made a promise to remain the best of friends, before getting married, no matter what happened in the future; and we kept that promise. It was important to us to remain friends, for the sake of raising happy, healthy, well-balanced children, despite our marital status. James always continued to be a great friend, a wonderfully supportive and engaged father. For that, I will always be grateful.

Ironically, amid this breakup, we were in the middle of adopting a teenager. Her name was Melissa, who would become our eldest child, as she was 10 years older than Kelly. I used to babysit Melissa when I was a teenager, and she was a young child. After some years of being out of contact, I found her in a group home, as she had been taken away from her mother for child abuse and child neglect. That's what prompted James and I to pursue adoption. In the meantime, we were granted visitation privileges that allowed Melissa to spend weekends and several weeks during the summer with us, as a family. Of course, the courts did not know of our recent separation.

Melissa had a roommate at the group home who spent a lot of time with us, as well. We attempted to adopt her too, but there were legal circumstances which did not permit us to move forward. However, we developed such a close child-parent relationship that we accepted Maria as our second oldest daughter anyway. That is how I managed to get myself the big family I had always dreamed of – five kids - four daughters and a son.

Shortly after the separation, the children and I moved into a rental house that my Uncle Tony owned on Cottage Grove in Cleveland Heights. James was hired by the local police department and moved in with his girlfriend. The house on Cottage Grove was a large three-story house with five bedrooms, two bathrooms, a living room, dining room, sunroom, kitchen, and basement. I had more than enough space for all of us, but my hands were more than full!

The children's ages ranged from 1 to 15 and they each had their own set of wants, needs, and challenges. Of course, the teenage girls helped with their younger siblings, but even still, it was overwhelming. I was a single parent, a college dropout, and desperately missing the love of my life, Jim. While I was moving forward in my journey, Jim had gone through seminary, took the oath of celibacy, and was ordained a Catholic priest – just like he said he would do! I did the only thing I knew to do to cope, and that was to drink. I kept a supply of White Zinfandel in the fridge and drank daily. I had to drink to deal with my life, my children, my job, my loss of love, and every other aspect of life. I was alone in this process, in over my head, and I needed help.

Thank God for Darlene! I called my best friend from high school, explained my situation, and begged her to move in with me and help me with the children. You guessed it! She said yes, and three days later showed up with all her belongings! Darlene moved into the bedroom next to mine, on the third floor of the house, where we shared a bathroom. The younger children shared one of the three bedrooms on the second floor, and the teenage girls shared the room across the hall from them. That left one spare bedroom, which would serve as a guest room, and it was put to good use, as well.

I was in the habit of taking in people and stray animals. In hindsight, that was due to the overwhelming loneliness I felt as a child; I had a desperate need to add to my household, to feel valued as a person. I wanted and needed to care for and nurture others to feel a real sense of purpose. Undoubtedly, I was putting a Band-Aid on the real issue, but it felt good and made me feel a sense of self-worth.

Chapter 6 – The Struggle

Looking back to that first drink, in West Virginia, at 15 years old…that was the beginning of the struggle. I innocently took that first drink, and the drink took me. I drank in excess from day one and could never successfully manage my liquor. I started out having an enjoyable time, being social, and just being an adult – oh, that's right, I wasn't an adult until six years later (at least not of legal drinking age)! Doesn't everyone drink to the point of blacking out while in college? I thought that was the very definition of having fun! There was just something different about my drinking – I could not seem to get enough – I didn't have an off switch. I could not stop unless I was pregnant. My desire to be a good mom outweighed my desire to drink – Wasn't that God doing for me that which I couldn't do for myself?

Once I had Marissa, I had completed my contribution to society – I was done having kids! I had five children, and I was happy. I was a fulltime mom, with a son and four daughters, who were each special in their own way. We had even taken in a dog that would not bark and didn't like to go outside, so he fit right in – just as dysfunctional as the rest of us! We had Darlene to help take care of us all, and that allowed me room to drink even more (but not in front of the younger children). Darlene had the little ones on an extremely strict schedule and that required my drinking to wait until after 9pm, when they went to bed. The older girls were allowed to stay up later, which in turn caused them to first witness our drinking and parties, and later to join us in the festivities. I am not proud of the fact that I allowed my teenage daughters to drink with me, however, I share this with transparency so you can understand the depths to which problem drinking can take you.

At this point, I did not realize that I was crossing the line into full blown alcoholism; I thought I might just drink a little too much from time to time. I did not think the irrational decisions, suicide attempts, and hospitalizations were that big of a deal. They only happened on occasion – so I thought. Thank God for Darlene because without her, I would surely have lost custody of my children. She held it together when I could not. She was the glue to my nuclear family at the time, not me. Again, God doing for me what I couldn't do for myself.

My drinking often caused me to be emotionally absent from my children, and my family, even when I was physically present. No one understood me, as no one had spent a day in my shoes. But, in the Confident Woman Devotional, on August 19th, Joyce Meyer teaches us that "Jesus understands us when nobody else does. He even understands us when we don't understand ourselves." I knew my family and friends loved me, whether they understood me or not, but I stayed away from them during the worst of my drinking, so as not to expose myself as the sick human being that I had become.

I even tried a geographical cure – I moved to Columbus, Ohio (without Darlene) thinking I was okay and could manage on my own, but that turned out to be a complete debacle. I ended up being the victim of a volatile domestic violence relationship that wounded me physically, emotionally, and spiritually. The final limit was the night I was thrown across my living room, injuring discs L-4 and L-5 in my back. That is when I said enough is enough, waited for my abuser to go to work, packed up my kids, and found myself running back home to Cleveland.

Of course, my family welcomed me home with open arms, as they were relieved that I had not been killed while living in Columbus. By this time, the older girls, Melissa, and Maria, were on their own, Kelly was entering eighth grade, William and Marissa were in elementary school. Life evened out for us, at least for a little while. I seemed to have gotten things back to normal and in a fairly good place. My drinking slowed down, and I spent more quality time with the children and family.

Just as things were starting to get back to normal, and I had decided to stop drinking, go to treatment for the first time, and start taking better care of myself and my family, I had a revelation that was the first of several that turned my family upside down. It was always something! I had been sober but for a brief time and was actively working on my 12-step recovery program with my first sponsor, Alesia. Things seemed to be going so well. I had completed my first three steps, glanced over the remainder of the steps, and decided I would skip down to step nine and begin making my amends. I was gung-ho about doing this recovery thing right and I wanted to correct all my wrongs, as soon as possible. That was a mistake. The twelve steps of recovery are in order, for a reason. Being newly sober, and not thinking of consulting anyone for advice, I stepped into an area of my life that I was not prepared to handle.

A few years prior to that time, it had been brought to my attention, by one of my cousins, that my son very strongly resembled someone she knew I had previously dated off and on, prior to James and I moving in together. She was visiting one of her relatives, who was also a relative of Terance, the young man I had dated off and on for several years. While visiting her aunt and uncle, she saw an elementary school picture of Terance hanging on the wall and thought she was looking at a picture of my son! That prompted her to immediately contact me and question me as to the paternity of my child. Of course, I was taken aback and thought it only coincidental, at first. But after really thinking back, I realized it was entirely possible for Terance to be my son's biological father! Oh my God! What was I to do? William was about 10 years old at the time. Riddled with fear, still drinking, and not knowing this to be a fact, I decided to silently sit on the possibility, until I gathered more concrete information and courage.

Over the next few years, well after James and I divorced, I generically introduced William to Terance, as a close friend of mine that wanted to take him to football games and hang out a little, since he was the only boy in the house. That worked for a little while, but it became more and more evident that they were biologically related. In addition to a very close resemblance, their body types were nearly identical, the depth of their voices, and many of their mannerisms very, very similar. It was scary and incredible to witness their natural affinity for one another, and it simply became undeniable that they were father and son.

The turn of the century had come and gone, mostly without incident except for the tornado that was about to become my life, and the life of everyone who loved or cared about me. Being the overly zealous rookie in recovery, and having all the evidence I thought I needed, I decided it was time to confess this situation of wrongful paternity, first to William, then to James, and finally to the remainder of my family. You can only imagine the wreckage that was caused, most importantly for William, James, and Terance; but also, for me, my parents, my uncles, and my daughters. Everyone was shocked, upset, disappointed, angry, and deeply hurt.

Until that time, I had never been directly responsible for hurting so many people and turning so many lives upside down. William was beyond shocked and bewildered, as I blurted out that James was not his biological father. We were standing in our driveway, after William had returned home from an outing with a friend. I can hardly believe that I asked him to guess who his father was, instead of just telling him! That was so insensitive! I'm so sorry, William!

James was understandably enraged, after raising and working so hard to support this child financially and emotionally for his entire young life. Terance expressed feeling cheated out of the fatherhood he was entitled to, yet grateful for the amazing job James had done in legally being William's father. The irony of James and I deciding to marry as the direct result of me being pregnant with William only added fuel to the fire, for perhaps absent from that pregnancy, or certainly had the truth been known, we probably would never have married.

That familial debacle took more than a year to find its way back to some semblance of normalcy, and I found my way back to the bottle. Of course, the family dynamic would forever be different, as it included William having two dads, James and Terance. But, in time, we were able to all be in a room together, without proverbial gunfire, and everyone exercised a level of acceptance that allowed us to coexist. If only I could find a way to forgive myself, stay sober, and move forward with my life.

I soon found myself in another long-term relationship that started out healthy, and fun, but ended horribly, with infidelity, and heartbreak. It's not even worth going into the details, just suffice it to say I just couldn't seem to get it right. I often asked God why He was allowing me to experience all these challenges? What had I done to deserve such a difficult life? Okay, maybe that's not a fair question, as my adult life had been full of chaos and perhaps, I deserved everything I was getting. Afterall, karma is real, right? I saw many of my friends' living life to the fullest and with what appeared to be so much joy; why couldn't I have that?

But I soon realized that I did have joy, in the midst of the storm, because I had finally stopped drinking again, went back to treatment, and got sober again. My family felt whole, despite the incidents of the past and the recently broken relationship. I was in early sobriety by the time Marissa and William were in high school, and I certainly didn't know a lot, but I knew enough to not drink when faced with the difficulties of life. I knew enough to work the steps in order, call my sponsor every day and when I found myself feeling anxious. I knew to lean on my Higher Power to get through the tough times, and it's a good thing I did, because those times were right around the corner...again.

During early sobriety, and as that last relationship was spiraling out of control, I was diagnosed with cancer; and to add insult to injury, both my daughters, Kelly (21) and Marissa (15) were pregnant! I was so scared! Kelly was in her first year of law school, and Marissa was a sophomore in high school. What was I to do? I needed to live to see these grandbabies – hell, I needed to live to help them, especially Marissa!

I remember the phone call, as if it were just yesterday. The doctor told me I had stage three breast cancer and that we would need to start treatment right away. My knees buckled as I stood in my kitchen, and I began to weep. Instinctively, I knew to call my sponsor, Detra. I called

Detra and we cried on the phone together for about five minutes; then she told me to stop crying because we needed to get into the solution for this problem! She asked what the doctor said, and I told her that I would need to have chemotherapy, surgery, and radiation. She promised to go with me for my first chemo treatment, and for as many more as necessary. That was an especially tough phone call, but my sponsor got me through it – God doing for me what I couldn't do for myself. Then, I was able to call my mom.

Mom, Kelly, and Detra accompanied me to my first chemotherapy treatment. I was terrified. I felt like a laboratory rat that was about to be given rat poison. We got into the room; the nurse had me change into a little gown that was more like a shirt and she left the room to get my Oncologist. The doctor came into the room and, with tears streaming down my cheeks, I announced that I had decided against the chemotherapy. I was too scared! I asked her how long I might have to live without the chemo, and she stated, "Maybe a year." I told her that would be fine and asked to get dressed to go home. My mother began to weep, as did my daughter and me.

My sponsor politely asked everyone to leave the room so she could have a word with me. She insisted that I was going to take the chemotherapy treatment, and she would not allow me to be that selfish! She reminded me that I had parents and children to live for and that I had to at least give it a good fight! She acknowledged and validated my fear, but she was not letting me leave that room without agreeing to have the treatment.

I listened to Detra and completed all my chemotherapy before having a successful surgery, followed by several rounds of radiation. I was especially grateful that I had so much support during that tough time, as my family was there, along with Detra, and Father Jim, who always kept tabs on me and the kids, despite my relationship status. He was always truly a friend who never stopped loving me in the purest sense of the word. I thank God for him, and I thank God for Detra, as He used them all to save my life. Detra, along with Darlene and my parents are the four people to whom I literally owe my life. I thank God for them every day.

I may not have had everything I thought I wanted or deserved, but I did have something phenomenal; I had my life, my sobriety; my parents, and my amazing children! The youngest three all graduated from high school early (in spite of me); Kelly went on to college and then to law school in Buffalo, New York; William moved across the country to Los Angeles, California to start his adult life and career; Marissa went to college in Buffalo, with her sister. Melissa and Maria were off being young adults, raising my eldest grandchildren, and independently living their lives to the best of their abilities. I beat the cancer with flying colors and was fully present for the birth of both of my grandsons, Jay and Chase! Again, God doing for me what I couldn't do for myself!

While God was working things out in my life, the eldest daughters were navigating life to the best of their abilities, yet not withstanding some of the vicissitudes that life had to offer. Melissa was battling her own demons of addiction, while Maria was faced with the challenges of being a single parent and trying to provide the best possible life for her daughter. We were all dealing with our own personal issues while trying to support one another to the best of our abilities.

Chapter 7 – There is a God

July 1, 2003, was the day I was granted a new life, a second chance, an opportunity to fulfill my potential, achieve my wildest dreams, and live my best life! God blessed me to live two lives in one lifetime, and for that I will be forever grateful. July 1, 2003, is my sobriety date. From that day to this one, I have experienced the blessing of uninterrupted sobriety. I have not found it necessary to pick up a drink, or any other mood- or mind-altering substance. This has been a gift from God; one which I can never repay, as it is only by God's grace and mercy that I am sober today.

My journey through sobriety has been challenging, interesting, humorous, and different, but mostly amazing. It has been the perfect platform to get to know myself and solidify my relationship with God. Recovery has taught me how to love myself and others, and how to be of maximum service to God and my fellow man, woman, and child. Twelve step recovery is a program for living that could benefit just about anyone (with or without addictions). It is a beautiful way of living that has positive effects on the individual, their family, and their community. And because of the concept of one person helping another, it has exponential effects well beyond the confines of one's own immediate sphere of influence – it's wide-reaching, sometimes all the way across the world!

Our textbook tells us that we are people who normally wouldn't mix, but there is a special fellowship among us that causes us to identify and relate to the experiences and feelings associated with alcoholism and addiction. We first come together due to a common peril, but we stay together because of a common solution. We must help and support one another, or we risk not staying sober ourselves. What a concept?!? Who would have thought of one sick person helping another, to get better and stay that way for an extended period? Believe me, as counterintuitive as it sounds, it really does work.

It all started just prior to my sobriety date, in late June 2003, as I was in rough shape and needed to detox and go to treatment again. I was blessed to have my medical care and beginnings at a world-renowned hospital, the Cleveland Clinic, in Cleveland, Ohio. It was a difficult, but necessary, choice to enter detox and submit myself to the care of others, as I found my way to July 1, 2003. I must admit that I wasn't the most pleasant and cooperative patient, but the fog did eventually begin to lift – at least enough for me to realize that I had nowhere else to go, if I were to continue existing on this planet.

My doctor pointed out to me that every time I ended up in the psychiatric unit for a suicide attempt, it had been within 72 hours (about 3 days) of taking a drink. That revelation made a lightbulb come on in my head. This was really a serious, life or death, situation that needed to be dealt with and it had to start with detox and then total abstinence from any alcohol, mood, or mind-altering substances. I didn't know how I was to manage without alcohol. I didn't know how I would ever have fun or socialize again. All I knew was that I wanted to live, and I wanted the emotional pain to stop. That is called the gift of desperation.

In my first year of sobriety, I had participated in every treatment program offered by Cleveland Clinic, sought outside therapy, and participated in a relapse prevention group for women. I had two sponsors, Alesia and Detra, started going to 12-step meetings again, making new friends, and hanging out at what we call "new playgrounds". I no longer went to bars. I avoided the beer aisle at the grocery store, and I started drinking a lot of coffee. I was scared to death of relapsing, so I attended 10-15 meetings a week, talked to at least one of my sponsors nearly every day, and read everything I could get my hands on about recovery. My sponsor Alesia re-started me on my first three steps, and my sponsor Detra took over and got me through the remainder of the 12 steps. Alesia took me to women's luncheons and international conferences, while Detra was the "AA Police" who dealt with me on a more day-to-day basis. I truly had the best of both worlds for recovery sponsorship, and for that I will be eternally grateful.

I guess you could say I was riding the proverbial pink cloud during that first year, but that nearly came to a screeching halt during my second year of sobriety. Life started to get real; it started to get really hard; and it forced me to really lean into my program of recovery. That is when the cancer diagnosis happened. That is when the girls were pregnant with Jay & Chase. That was a terrifying time in my life, but I never thought of taking a drink. I never considered jeopardizing my sobriety due to having a life-threatening illness. If anything, I wanted that much more to be strong, fight for my life, stay sober, and meet my grandsons. The boys were born about six weeks apart – two healthy, bouncing baby boys. I thank God for allowing me to be present for both of their miraculous entrances into the world. That was the beginning of many blessings that were bestowed upon me in this rollercoaster called life in sobriety.

Life did not suddenly become "a bed of roses," but it did allow me to deal with the good and bad, on life's terms, and without the need or desire to take a drink. I adopted a level of acceptance that afforded me peace, in the midst of the storm, even when the storm was raging, painful, and scary. It wasn't long after the boys were born that my Nanny passed away. She was the first person in my family, whom I had been particularly close to, that died, and her passing was extremely difficult. There was a time when I first got sober that I believed I wouldn't be able to stay sober if I lost my grandmother, but when that time came, I was surrounded by friends and family and, amazingly, never thought about having a drink! I believe the challenging events that occurred during my early recovery, coupled with being deeply entrenched in the program, afforded me the opportunity to really begin to live life, to check some things off my bucket list, explore this country, navigate the challenges of life, and establish a strong foundation for my sobriety.

After Nanny had passed away, and just as I was approaching my sixth year in recovery, I decided to relocate from Cleveland, Ohio to Greensboro, North Carolina, where my father lived. It was time to do something different, in a new environment, and spend some quality time with my father, younger sister, Pat, and my niece and nephews. Of course, it was a little scary, as my recovery had been deeply rooted in Cleveland, but I considered myself a big girl who was ready to branch out into the world and see what life had to offer, outside of my hometown. I also got permission from my sponsor, Detra, before leaving!

Greensboro had a lot to offer. I had family, made friends in recovery, found my next husband, and went back to school, after more than 30 years. I stayed in Greensboro for five years and the quality time spent with my father, stepmom, sister, niece, and two nephews was invaluable. My program of recovery reached new heights, as I began to sponsor young women and help them through the 12 steps of recovery. The time and energy spent on helping them stay sober was not just helping them, but it was enhancing my recovery experience exponentially, as well.

At one point, I had seven sponsees, and we were truly like a family. As a matter of fact, people called us the Bear Family because I was the Mama Bear with my seven little cubs, and we spent lots of time together in meetings, conferences, BBQ's, and other recovery-centered events. I love and miss each, and every, one of those women, as they were a significant part of my life. I believe God had most of those women come into my life for a season, while others were for a lifetime; but regardless, they were all intentionally placed in my life at the perfect time.

One of my sponsees who falls into the lifetime category is named Runt. I call her Runt because she was the youngest in sobriety of all the other women that I sponsored. She was my baby cub that I gave a little extra time and attention because she needed it. Runt felt most like one of my daughters, and I am not afraid to admit that I have always held a very special place in my heart for her. My advice to Runt, and her sponsee sisters, was always to do what was in front of them; do the next right thing, and when they didn't know what else to do, reach out to me (or someone else in recovery), get to a meeting, and don't pick up a drink! Runt, you know I loved you then, I love you now, and I'll love you for all eternity!

Speaking of love, I managed to find that in Greensboro too. Shortly after my arrival, in a meeting at the local recovery club, I met Chap. He had just celebrated his first year of sobriety and was on fire for the program. His story was incredible, as he had overcome many obstacles and barriers in life yet managed to achieve and maintain sobriety. It was remarkable! He had been drinking since he was, literally, a baby, as his parents' put alcohol in his bottle to get him to sleep, and he drank from that point forward … until the day he went to treatment for his alcoholism and found his way into the program of recovery. Needless to say, I was more than impressed. I was enamored and thought I could enhance his life by exposing him to things he never had the opportunity to experience, take him places he had never been (he hadn't been much of anywhere outside of Greensboro), and show him a lifestyle that would change his life forever…and I did that.

We married at the very clubhouse where we met, exactly one year from the day of our first date – July 1, 2010 (on my sobriety date). It was my 7th anniversary. He presented me with a special 7-year chip during the ceremony and we celebrated the occasion with almost 100 of our closest friends and family. Obviously, this was not my first go-round at marriage, so I was especially hopeful this would be the one that would stick. Though we didn't have much in common, outside of our sobriety, we were both hard-working, forward-thinking, on fire for recovery, and desperately wanted someone with which to share our lives; but he wasn't Father Jim, and the love didn't even begin to compare. I had pretty much given up on the idea of that kind of love ever becoming a reality again, so I chose to move on and settle for the best-case scenario, at the time. But would that be enough for a lasting, happy marriage? I hoped it would.

Naturally, things started out well. We started our lives together in a cute, modest little apartment. We spent lots of time together, went to meetings, and became the recovery power couple in Greensboro. He was very supportive of me in a variety of ways. He supported the time I spent with my sponsees, individually and collectively; he supported my desire for a career change; and he supported my efforts to get back into school to complete my undergraduate degree. In turn, I supported him by teaching him things he never learned as a child, elevating his vocabulary, increasing his general academic knowledge, and exposure to some of the finer things in life. We traveled – as a matter of fact he took his first airplane ride with me when I surprised him with a trip to Las Vegas! It was so much fun! Watching him experience the airport, the flights, and the Las Vegas experience was incredible. He was like a kid in a candy store!

I enrolled as a fulltime student at North Carolina A&T State University (NCAT) in the fall of 2011. Chap and I had agreed that I would complete my degree in Criminal Justice and then go to law school to become an attorney. The plan was for him to retire after I completed law school, passed the bar exam, and landed my first job as an attorney. I felt so blessed to have his full emotional and financial support to be able to complete my undergraduate degree and start to achieve some of the things I never thought possible. This was his way of demonstrating his love for me. He was willing to work two jobs so I could concentrate on attending and doing well in school, in preparation for getting accepted into law school. I truly appreciated him for his patience and sacrifice that was designed to benefit us in the future.

Chap's family was very supportive as well. I had developed a close relationship with his mom and 9 siblings, as they all lovingly welcomed me into the family and encouraged me in my goal to complete my undergraduate degree. I grew especially close to Chap's great-nephew, Antione. He was an impressionable, handsome, young teenager who seemed drawn to me upon our first meeting. We immediately established a close familial relationship, much like that of Chap's brothers, sisters, and other family members.

Life was basically going as planned as I approached the spring of 2014 and graduation. I graduated with honors and finally achieved the goal my mother had waited for me to achieve since I first graduated from high school. I completed my undergraduate degree, and we both knew that degree belonged to her!

In the meantime, Chap and I had experienced some of the challenges of marriage, but nothing earth-shattering – no deal breakers. He continued working hard while I applied to 17 law schools, got waitlisted at 4, accepted at 3, and offered scholarships at 2 - Southern University Law Center in Baton Rouge, Louisiana, and Florida A&M University (FAMU) College of Law in Orlando, Florida. Ultimately, I decided to attend FAMU, and we moved to Orlando three days after I graduated from NCAT.

Orlando was beautiful, hot, and humid. It was a different experience than Greensboro or Cleveland. There was so much to do, with Disney World, Universal Studios, University of Central Florida (UCF), shopping outlets, a million restaurants, FAMU College of Law, and more! Of course, most of my time was spent at FAMU and most of Chap's time was spent at Disney Springs, where he worked, as a chef, at one of the many restaurants just outside of Disney World.

We started out living in a little 800 square foot, efficiency apartment, with the smallest bathroom I had ever seen in my life, as the cost of living was quite a bit more expensive than either of us were accustomed. That lasted about 6 months before I started getting cabin fever, so we moved into a 1600 square foot, three-bedroom house shortly after I started law school. We were reasonably happy and moving on up!

My first semester of law school was, hands down, the most difficult academic experience of my lifetime. I started with seven challenging classes and did more reading than ever before in my life. And to add insult to injury, the students were graded against one another, in each class! The grading system made it mandatory for a small percentage of students to earn A's, while a small percentage were doomed to failure (everyone else fell somewhere in the middle). I had always heard of the highly competitive nature of law school, medical school, and business school, but I didn't really understand it, until I found myself on the firing line!

I can admit law school to be far more challenging than my undergraduate studies, and there were many times when I felt I wouldn't successfully complete my first year (1L); but as fate would have it, I managed to complete not only the first semester, but the first year with average grades. It was an ego-deflating academic experience, as I was previously accustomed to performing in the top percentage of my class, as opposed to being in the middle of the pack. For law school, I had to learn to strive for excellence, yet accept the reality of the situation, and just keep pushing towards completion. It was a hard pill to swallow, but what choice did I have?

By the time I became a 2L at FAMU, several things had begun to change at home. Some things were good, some were just different, and others were not so good. To start, we accidentally stumbled across an opportunity to move, yet once again, to a larger, more luxurious home in a more exclusive neighborhood. Chap had first said we were not moving, as we had only been in our house a few months, but he agreed to go see the new house. As soon as he stepped two feet into the house, he said, "We'll take it!" It was the deal of the century, so we jumped all over it, packed up and moved in. The house was just shy of 3000 square feet, with 4 bedrooms, 3 bathrooms, 2 family rooms, living room, dining room, kitchen, and a large, covered in-ground swimming pool! It was beautiful and a dream come true! I remember Chap and I asking ourselves what were we going to do with all the space, considering it was just the two of us in the household? We figured we would simply enjoy the space and amenities, and let God figure it out for us!

Shortly after moving into the new house, we found a wonderful church home at New Life Church of Orlando and began attending Sunday services and Wednesday Night Bible Study regularly. Chap immediately became very involved in various ministries within the church, and once the pastor found out he was a chef, Chap began preparing breakfast for the congregation every week before Sunday School. Life was full and Sunday breakfast was fun and delicious! From time to time, we would have the pastoral staff and 20-30 members of the congregation over for dinner, following Sunday service. It is safe to say we were well-received, well-respected, and well-liked at New Life Church.

Unfortunately, I was beginning to feel that my husband didn't like me as much at home as he did at church. He was like Dr. Jekyll and Mr. Hyde in that way. At church he was loving, kind, and considerate, and by the time we got to the church parking lot, following Sunday service, he was cussing me out, and speaking to me in a hurtful and demeaning manner. He had become very controlling and constantly reminded me of his requirement that I follow biblical principles and fully submit to his decisions and desires, without question, 100% of the time. It was as if I were not to have a mind of my own because of being a woman. He was very clear in his demand that I respect his authority, and that meant all decisions were ultimately his to make. In his mind, it was my duty to silently comply, regardless of my opinion and how I may have felt about a situation.

It was becoming unbearable, and I knew something had to change. My serenity and sobriety were at risk, as I was only attending AA meetings once or twice a month, trying to do well in law school, and trying my best to be a good wife, because I didn't want another failed marriage. I prayed, I lost 40 pounds and spent lots of late nights in the swimming pool crying, but nothing seemed to help.

That is, until we got a desperate phone call from Chap's teenage nephew, Antione, with whom I had previously developed a close familial relationship. He wanted to leave Greensboro and come to Orlando to live with us. He had was in the middle of his junior year of high school and felt in jeopardy of dropping out of school, like most of his family members, if he didn't change his environment. Knowing of my privileged upbringing and recent academic accomplishments, Antione figured he would have a greater chance of graduating if he were in our care.

Antione was right and there was nothing stopping us from being able to care for him, as we certainly had the willingness and the space! I'm sure God was laughing about us being worried about what to do with all that space! While we thought we had been blessed with this beautiful, spacious house for ourselves, God had something else in mind, all along! I thought this change was just what we needed, someone else on which to focus and set a good example. We didn't have any children together, so Antione sort of became our "kid" and we needed to be on our best behavior as "parents". Could this have been the answer to my prayers?

So far, so good...with the pastor's help, we got Antione enrolled in a private school, the church choir, and exposed him to the youth group at church. That went smoothly and things at home seemed to begin to improve. It was such a pleasure having Antione in the house. He was loving, kind, considerate, funny, and he loved his Auntie Angel. It was so fulfilling to be able to directly impact the life of a child who had been so disadvantaged. Along with exposing Chap to a better life, I was able to help expose Antione to a new life full of possibilities and opportunities.

Chapter 8 – It Gets Worse Before It Gets Better

Antione's matriculation through high school went relatively well. He was the star of the basketball team, doing reasonably well academically, and was well-adapted to life in Florida with his extended family. He loved it! Antione was well on his way to becoming one of the few high school graduates in his family. His junior year was winding down and my second year of law school was ending. I was looking forward to getting a break from school during the summer, as I was also working as a certified domestic violence advocate at Harbor House of Central Florida, the local domestic violence awareness agency in Orlando.

If only I had read my devotional (or had a crystal ball) before starting that day – the day that would forever change my life, and the life of my entire family; I would have better prepared; I could have braced myself, or perhaps done something to awaken from, what had to be, the scariest of nightmares – the one from which you long to wake up, but cannot. Perhaps I could have changed the outcome of the day, and the very trajectory of our lives, if only I could have awakened. What if I had awakened? What if it was all just a bad dream? What if?

That was the question I asked myself, over, and over again, as the day began to unfold. What if only I had done this; or if only I had done that? Would this be happening, if only I had not been so nurturing and loving? Should I have been more rigid, as a parent? Might things have turned out differently, had I not made some of the mistakes of my youth, as a parent, or had I graduated from college, right out of high school? I had so many questions! I felt, somehow, this had to be my fault! There must have been some way I could have prevented this; after all, I am a mother, the single most important job in the world! As a mother, my primary responsibility is to protect my children, and I have failed miserably. Life, as I knew it, would never again be the same.

It was no ordinary day. In fact, it was a day for celebration. Upon awakening, I was only a few hours away from boarding an airplane headed to my hometown of Cleveland, Ohio, to meet my mother, son, daughters, grandchildren, and even my super-cop, ex-husband to begin the caravan to Ithaca, New York the following morning. We were going to witness my daughter, Kelly's graduation from Cornell University's SC Johnson College of Business. She had earned her MBA (with accolades, of course) and just returned from her study abroad program in South Africa. This was a busy and exciting day; one of those that makes a mother proud!

The early part of the morning was unusually quiet in the office, which allowed more time for us girls to chat; and of course, I took the opportunity to brag about my kids; especially the one graduating. She is such a smart cookie, but then again, all my children are special – all five of them. They have their own unique gifts and talents; and in their own way, they are all a little crazy too! Of course, they would say "The apple doesn't fall far from the tree, Mom!"

Days like these often cause us to pause and reflect upon our journey in this complicated game of life. Various situations and circumstances cause us to question our life choices; in some instances, even second-guessing what we thought were good ideas or decisions. The truth is, we can question ourselves, or doubt ourselves all day long, but it will not change a thing. What is done is done. Now we must learn from our actions, and the consequences of our decisions, whatever they may be; and move on.

This was one of those days. This was a day which required deep reflection and review of my life, in its entirety; specifically for the purpose of attempting to pinpoint the place, or time, in which I had gone wrong; for I desperately needed to know. What choices or decisions had led me to this deep, dark moment in time, when I heard the fourteen worlds that would change my life forever? ***"Your daughter has been shot in the head, and she's in surgery right now."***

Life, as I knew it, would never again be the same. I had experienced any mother's worst nightmare. Someone tried to kill my child; my youngest child; my baby girl; the child I carried in my womb and raised from a baby; the child I saw take her first steps and heard say her first words. Someone tried to take Marissa away from me, away from us, away from her children. My grief and horror simply could not be contained. As the words came out of my mother's mouth, I let out a blood-curdling scream on the airplane. I could not believe what I was hearing. I sobbed uncontrollably, while fellow passengers attempted to console me. The precious woman sitting next to me began to pray, which was something I could not even think to do, at that very moment. After about ten minutes, the crew let me off the plane first, and I ran through the airport to the nearest restroom, locked myself in a stall and wailed out to God, asking why this had happened and begged Him to please save my baby girl.

On the surface, I would have felt that not to be a real prayer, and instead more of a venting and bargaining session with God; but in retrospect, I recognize it was the deepest form of prayer; one which required one-hundred percent dependence upon God, and zero percent dependence upon self. It is not often we find ourselves in prayer with that amount of depth and weight, but that is what God wants from us; that is what My Father wants from me – every day.

My Uncle Mike picked me up from the airport in Akron, Ohio and took me directly to the hospital where my daughter was in surgery fighting for her life. That 45-minute ride seemed to take hours, as I was so anxious to see my child. When I arrived at Metro Hospital, my sponsor, Detra and her girlfriend, Terry, were there, along with my ex-husband James and his wife. We all hugged and cried; we waited, and waited for what seemed to be an eternity, for Marissa to come out of surgery. Finally, the doctor appeared, and I stopped breathing. Did she make it? Would she be, okay? What was happening?

On that particular day, May 26th, my Sarah Young devotional entitled *Jesus Calling*, warned me of the evil of the world, reminding me of the stability, omniscience, and omnipotence of My Father, while encouraging me to lean upon Him, for my strength. Little did I know just how much I would need that strength, that day, and all the days to follow.

Marissa had come through the surgery, with flying colors! She was literally unrecognizable, but if she made it through the next few days, the doctors felt she would survive. I prayed like never before, and in the midst of one of my prayers, Father Jim walked into the waiting room. Thank God! Of course, he was there to support me and the family in such a time of need! That was his M.O. Though he admittedly still loved me, he never interfered in my life, or relationships; but he was always there when we needed him. Would it be possible to ever experience that kind of long-lasting, unconditional love, from a man, again?

The days, weeks, and months to follow were beyond challenging. My daughter was still fighting for her life; I had obtained temporary, emergency custody of her two children, moved them with me to Florida, and returned to law school for my second-year final exams. Thank goodness summer was upon us, as it provided a little time to get things together for the children and our newfound lives. I enrolled the children in elementary and middle school, resigned from my job, and poured my heart and soul into grandparenting, and my final year of law school.

As Marissa began to recover in Cleveland, with the support of her father and stepmother, the children and I tried to focus on our academics, counseling, church, and their extracurricular activities. Mya took gymnastics and aerial silks, while Chase played basketball. Both children were active in church, sang in the youth choir, participated in the puppet ministry, while Mya danced with the praise dance team. To say we were busy was an understatement, as I still don't understand how there were enough hours in a day to do all that we were doing! It felt surreal, as if I was watching myself run around like a chicken without a head! Today I know it was only God's grace and mercy that gave me the strength and tenacity to walk through each day, cook, clean, eat, sleep, study, do laundry, help with homework, and do it all again the next day.

By Christmastime that year, Marissa had miraculously recovered enough to get her doctor's permission to fly to Orlando, and we had an amazing and special, warm Florida Christmas holiday. Just having her in my presence, walking, talking, laughing, loving, and hugging her children, was the best Christmas gift ever! Despite not having the entire family together (we were missing my son and the older girls), we shared a beautiful holiday with Chap, Antione, my mother, the younger girls, and their children. It turned out to be a very special Christmas for us all, including Antione who had not previously experienced such holiday fanfare, and Marissa who had a new outlook on and appreciation for life. We were all tremendously blessed.

The next 21 months proved to be quite difficult, as my marriage was falling apart at the seams, mostly due to the level of control Chap was exerting, along with his insistence on relinquishing the children to some other family members. He claimed to care for them but felt he had not signed up to raise children when he met and married me. He wanted me all to himself, and simply did not want me sharing my time and attention with anyone. I tried to explain that this undertaking was due to a family emergency beyond our control and remind him that we had taken in his nephew, prior to my daughter's near-death experience, to offer him the opportunity of a better life. My efforts were futile. He just couldn't see that it was fair and reasonable that we help Chase and Mya, in their time of need, just like we helped Antione, in his time of need. Of course, as the grandmother of these children, it was my desire and responsibility to step in and fill the shoes of my daughter, under such serious circumstances. What kind of mother would I have been to simply say, "I'm sorry, there's nothing I can do!" There was no way I was doing that, as I knew I was operating within the will of God, and nothing was going to convince me to forego the wellbeing of my grandchildren! I guess I just had to be the disobedient wife who chose to listen to God. Fortunately, all the children in the household got along well and genuinely cared for one another, so that was sort of the silver-lining to the situation. The only person unhappy with our family dynamic was Chap; the rest of us were reasonably happy, especially when he wasn't home. Sorry Chap!

Antione graduated the following May and decided to return to Greensboro. He couldn't take seeing me so unhappy, and he felt his uncle didn't want him around anymore. Against all odds, I graduated the following December and started working for a local law firm. The marriage continued to deteriorate, but I was trying my best to hang in there. I couldn't fathom the idea of another divorce. I felt like such a failure! I had to make this marriage work!

By God's grace, Marissa continued to improve and came to visit us in Orlando several more times. That was especially challenging the last couple of visits because Chap was so difficult and got to the point where he didn't want her around. Hell, he didn't want any of us around! Things were spiraling out of control, and I could see the escalation could potentially become dangerous. I was miserable and afraid, the children were beginning to be affected, and my peace of mind had flown out of the nearest window. That was the straw that broke the camel's back for me! My peace of mind is nonnegotiable! After I have done all that I can do, I will do whatever it takes to recapture my peace and serenity. I will go to any length to protect my sobriety, and if that means I must walk away from a toxic situation, then so be it!

That's where things landed in September of the following year. I had had all that I could take. The children and I packed up a few of our belongings, got on a plane, and flew back to Cleveland with Marissa. It was only days after she had come to Orlando to celebrate Chase's 13th birthday. That was the beginning of the end – the end of life with Chap – the end of life in Florida – the end of being married – the end of having companionship – the end of life as I knew it.

As necessary as that decision was, I couldn't help but feel that life had just come to a screeching halt, and I would forevermore be miserable, lonely, and alone. Once again, I thought, I should have married Jim (before he became a Catholic priest), and maybe I wouldn't be going through this hell! I felt as if I were being punished for all the mistakes I had ever made, throughout my entire lifetime. I thought God was angry with me and therefore punishing me. Then I questioned whether I had made a mistake by leaving, and whether Chap was right about me needing to listen, do as I was told, and be a good, submissive wife. I wondered if I should turn around and go back, beg for forgiveness, and bend over beyond backwards to make things work?

My self-esteem was so low; I don't think it had ever been lower. I was on the verge of a very deep depression. I kept looking back at my life and all the failed relationships, relationships that would never have existed had Jim and I had the support of our parents and moved forward with our wedding plans at the quaint little chapel on the Ohio University campus decades earlier. I wondered if I would ever recover from that monumental mistake. When in doubt, call mom.

Thank God for Mom. I went directly to my mom's house, from the airport, to cry on her shoulder and got all the support and courage I needed to start over, with dignity and grace. I cried, talked, slept, reconnected with my friends in recovery in Cleveland, and prepared to face the rest of my life…still sober through it all.

Life back in Cleveland was challenging, but good for me. I was with my tribe, my family, and my friends. I went back to my recovery homegroup and picked up as if I had never left. I reconnected with old friends, made some new friends, and continued my life of uninterrupted sobriety, despite my circumstances. Life was a little bit lonely though, so I decided to get a dog. I rescued a beautiful, 100-pound, German Shepherd/Golden Retriever mix named Charlie.

Charlie was more than awesome! He loved me from the moment he laid eyes on me, and I felt the same way. Caring for Charlie became one of my main focuses in life – we did everything together. We traveled, played, and even danced together!

Unfortunately, Charlie was a bit too possessive, and protective of me and the family, as he bit my daughter's mover for walking into the house unannounced (he really should have knocked first). That incident cost me more than seven thousand dollars! Then, to add insult to injury. months later, Charlie attempted to bite two more people! He was out of control, and it left me no choice but to reluctantly surrender him. The liability was just too great. How that broke my heart! I cried all the way to the animal shelter and throughout the surrendering process. Charlie cried and I cried.

Once again, I thought I would never recover. But time heals **almost** all wounds, right? Time moved on and I slowly developed some acceptance around life without Charlie. It was lonely and difficult, but I made it through.

Chapter 9 – Dreams Do Come True

Life without Charlie was a stark contrast to the days when his presence filled the home with unspoken comfort. The house, once warm with the sounds of his gentle, but large footsteps and the quiet reassurance of his gaze, now felt cold and empty. The mornings were the hardest. Waking up to the silence where his soft breaths used to be, and the absence of his warm body nestled close by, was a constant reminder of the void left in his wake. There were moments when the grief seemed insurmountable, when the pain of his absence gnawed at the edges of joy, threatening to consume me entirely.

But in those moments of deepest despair, I found myself turning, as I always have, to the One who has never failed me. God, in His infinite wisdom, had prepared me for this, even if I hadn't seen it coming. His plan, so perfect in its unfolding, was beyond my understanding, but I trusted in His plan, nonetheless. For how many times had He carried me through the darkest valleys, only to lead me into the light on the other side? How many times had He taken the broken pieces of my life and crafted them into something beautiful, something that spoke of His love and grace?

I clung to the belief that God, in His all-knowing nature, had a purpose in everything. Even in the loss of Charlie, there was a lesson, a blessing yet to be revealed. It was a faith that had been tested and proven true countless times before. In the darkest moments of my life, when the weight of the world seemed too much to bear, it was God's strength that upheld me. It was His grace that sustained me, His mercy that comforted me. And it was in those very moments, when I had nothing left to give, that I learned the most valuable lesson of all: the less I depended on myself, and the more I leaned on Him, the better the outcome.

There were times when the situation seemed impossible, when the future looked bleak, and hope was but a flicker in the darkness. But time and time again, God showed me that He could take even the direst circumstances and transform them into something miraculous. His ability to turn tragedy into triumph, to bring beauty from ashes, was a testament to His boundless love and power. I saw it when I least expected it, in the quiet moments of prayer, in the whispered answers to my cries for help.

My life is a tapestry of these moments, each one a testament to God's unfailing love and His perfect plan. He has made my wildest dreams come true, even when everything around me seemed to be falling apart. There is a peace that comes with knowing that I am not in control, that I don't have to have all the answers. That peace is the gift of surrender, of laying down my burdens at the feet of the One who is more than capable of carrying them.

So, as I navigated life without Charlie, I did so with a heart full of gratitude—not just for the time I had with him, but for the knowledge that God was still at work, even in my pain. I am grateful for the constant reminders of His presence, for the ways He reveals His love, even in the smallest of details. And most of all, I am grateful that He is a God who sees me, who knows me, and who always has my best interest at heart, even when I don't know what's coming or what to do next.

Charlie's absence was a reminder of the fragility of life, but it was also a testament to the strength of my faith. And in that faith, I found a new kind of strength, one that could only come from complete dependence on my Heavenly Father. I am living proof that when we trust in God's plan, even the darkest days can be filled with hope, and even the deepest sorrow can be turned into joy.

As time passed and I began to heal emotionally, I found myself even more entrenched in recovery meetings. I needed to fill the void; I needed the support; I needed to be around people and be intentional about NOT isolating, in my grief, loneliness, and depression. I learned that early on in recovery – isolation is a very dangerous place to be, especially for a recovering alcoholic. I know that I need people; I need positivity; I need a different perspective to process my feelings and not to slip into a place of self-pity that could very possibly lead to a relapse.

That feeling of needing relief is very scary, because relief to this recovering alcoholic could spell W-H-I-T-E Z-I-N-F-A-D-E-L! One is too many and a thousand would never be enough! That's a road that doesn't need to be traveled – been there, done that, and got the t-shirt to prove it! I must protect my sobriety at all costs. Nothing, absolutely nothing, is worth taking a drink over, as it would only make things worse, never better. Praise God, I have been able to guard my sobriety with my life, no matter what the circumstances may be.

Staying sober has been such a gift – the gift that keeps on giving! I mentioned going to lots of recovery meetings, sharing openly and honestly, seeking the advice of my sponsor, and trying to help the next sick and suffering alcoholic. This is the behavior that, unbeknownst to me, would set me up for the next chapter of my life - The chapter that would change everything.

After returning to Cleveland and divorcing Chap, I threw myself into meetings with enthusiasm, fully embracing the opportunity to share, grow, heal, and understand myself better. In this journey of self-discovery and healing, I reconnected with Kenneth, from 17 years earlier, who quickly became my sobriety buddy and, soon after, my best friend in recovery.

Kenneth and I attended meetings together regularly, our paths intertwining more and more with each gathering. Afterward, we would share meals, deepening our connection over plates of comfort food that somehow tasted better because of the conversation that accompanied them. We watched movies and television series together, escaping into stories while creating our own narrative of friendship and recovery. Our conversations were rich with the value we placed on our sobriety, the lessons we were learning, and the heartaches and challenges that came with the journey. Through all of this, we grew closer, our bond strengthening as we both healed.

Kenneth had a presence that was impossible to ignore. He strolled into meetings with a calm, collected confidence that reminded me of "Cool Moe Dee," effortlessly cool with an air of peace around him. Kenneth was cute, yes, but it was his calm demeanor and collected nature that drew me in. Despite the unimaginable tragedies he had faced in his life and throughout his sobriety, he remained patient and loving, never letting his past dim his spirit. Instead, he used his experiences as a foundation for positivity, his upbeat attitude shining brightly in the face of adversity. He was unselfish, always quick to listen and slow to speak, finding humor in the little things and, most importantly, he was on fire for his sobriety.

Each time Kenneth strolled into the room, my heart would skip a beat. Even before I fully recognized it, I found myself smiling on the inside, the kind of smile that started deep within and slowly spread, warming me from the inside out. Those butterflies everyone talks about? I felt them fluttering around, delicate and insistent, but I fought those feelings, as my past was riddled with unhealthy relationships, the wounds of which were still fresh. I had sworn off the idea of giving my heart to another man, convinced that I would never again allow myself to be hurt like I had been before. I believed that my time for happiness had expired, and I was resigned to spending the rest of my life alone, safe from the pain that love had brought me.

But true love has a way of sneaking up on you, especially when you're not looking for it. Over time, it became clear that our relationship had hit a fork in the road, and it was changing rapidly. We were falling in love, despite my best efforts to guard my heart. We found that we rarely wanted to be apart, our time together becoming the highlight of our days.

It wasn't long before we had to acknowledge what was happening between us. The friendship we had built was transforming into something deeper, something more profound. We confessed our love for one another, the words spilling out as if they had been waiting a thousand years, and we both knew there was no turning back. With that confession came a commitment, a promise to be together no matter what. We got engaged and, in a whirlwind of love and certainty, we were married within weeks.

Looking back, I see God's hand in all of it. God protected me from my heartaches, bad experiences, unhealthy relationships and perhaps most importantly, He protected me from me, because sometimes I can be my own worst enemy. I was desperately searching for love, ever since the devastating end of what was to be the perfect union, at the tender age of 21, with Jim. I thought it impossible to ever love, or be loved like that again, so I searched and searched, unsuccessfully…until Kenneth came along. I had finally been blessed with the kind of love that had substance, depth, and weight – love that surpassed the unreachable bar that had been set 37 years earlier.

This was not my plan, nor was it Kenneth's plan, as I felt like damaged goods who could never truly love again, and Kenneth was a 61year-old, confirmed bachelor with no plans to ever marry! This was unequivocally God's plan, a divine blueprint that brought us together in a way that only He could orchestrate. He allowed us to develop a true friendship, to fall in love, and to be married, all within a timeline that seemed to defy reason, but felt entirely right.

On 2/2/22, we became husband and wife, and we are eternally grateful for the path that led us to that moment. Our union was created in love, nurtured by recovery, and blessed by God's grace. What began as a simple friendship in a recovery meeting blossomed into a love story that neither of us could have predicted, but one that we both cherish deeply. Praise God for His plans, which are always better than our own.

The past 31 months have truly been an adventure. Kenneth and I have lived in four different states, traveled across the country by car twice, attended recovery meetings in Cleveland, Twin Falls, Salt Lake City, Las Vegas, Baltimore, and Greensboro, and we have helped a myriad of people along the way. I told you; it's been an adventure!

Five months after our intimate nuptial celebration, we found ourselves on the first leg of our adventure, which involved packing up and driving 1900 miles across the United States to move from the Ohio to Idaho. I had accepted a challenging nonprofit leadership position in the beautiful city of Twin Falls, and yes, it was breathtakingly beautiful! The many mountains, canyons, rivers, and natural aesthetics were a sight to see, while the weather was similar to that of the Midwest (minus the excessive lake-effect snow during Cleveland winters).

Idaho, a very homogenous and conservative state, is large in size, but small in population, as there are just a little over a million people in the entire state. It was a bit of an adjustment, even culture shock, to become accustomed to the significant lack of diversity, racially and otherwise. For the most part, people were friendly and very polite, but there was always the question of why we were there. People just didn't understand, as it was quite apparent that we were outsiders.

After nearly two years in Idaho, Kenneth and I decided we needed to be closer to family and in a more diverse, welcoming environment, so we packed up, donated our furniture to Habitat for Humanity, and moved to Las Vegas, Nevada thinking it would be a great alternative, considering the ideal weather, diversity on many levels, family, and always having something fun to do! This was going to be the perfect destination!

Las Vegas has always been one of my favorite places on the planet (along with the Caribbean Islands and South Africa) – and let's just get it out of the way now; yes, I like to gamble… **just a little bit!** A good game of Free Bet Blackjack (it has the best odds), Three Card Poker, or High Card Flush are among my favorites.

The timing was perfect, I was about to celebrate my 60th birthday and we were in Las Vegas, so this became adventure number two. We spent time at Palms, Harrah's, the M Resort & Spa, and more (almost entirely comped)! We went to a variety of shows, ate at amazing restaurants, spent time with family and entertained our grandson, Chase, for his collegiate spring break. We even had breakfast with my childhood friend Rocky, and his wife Amy from Cleveland! We had a blast! That was the first three weeks…

Week four in Las Vegas was an absolute disaster! I thought I had landed a new job, so we started looking for a reasonable place to live. We thought we had found the perfect place that was run by people in recovery, so we anxiously went to look at it. I am almost speechless as I try to describe the horrendous conditions found at this allegedly sober, communal living complex. It takes my husband to accurately describe the conditions. He describes it as follows: "The stinking crypt of the dammed, smelled of death, with the sweet pungent smell of human remains. It was God-awful." That experience left my husband wondering how he could fix it so that no one would ever have to live in those conditions, as the stinking stench remained in his nostrils for three days. This was the part of Las Vegas we had never seen, nor imagined, before.

As God would have it, that job didn't work out after all, and left us wondering what was next? What would come of our second adventure? Where should we go? We had been in Las Vegas for nearly a month, and it was apparent that our time there had expired. Should we head back home to Cleveland, or should we continue the adventure, go to North Carolina to visit my dad and sister, Pat, and figure the rest out from there? Decisions, decisions, decisions…

Ken reminded me that we needed to pray. We needed to pray the prayer that got us to Idaho and led us to our next destination. The prayer was simple: "God, please send us where we can be of maximum service, wherever that may be." Secretly, I always wanted that to be somewhere warm and balmy, but I was willing to be obedient.

In addition to prayer and direction, we needed money to embark upon this eastward trip across the country. We were just about out of funds, as we anticipated me working withing a few weeks, so we solicited the assistance of our close family members, sold all our valuable possessions, including our treasured wedding rings, and began our journey across I-40 East headed to North Carolina.

It took us 4 days to drive across the country in two vehicles (during the day), and my dad was glad to see us when we finally arrived in Greensboro. But, more importantly, our prayer had been answered. Just as we crossed the border from Virginia into North Carolina, I got a message stating that I had been selected for a final interview to serve as Executive Director for a domestic violence awareness organization in North Carolina! Look at God!

Won't He do it?!? Here we are in beautiful Greensboro, North Carolina when I got the long-awaited call from Salisbury, North Carolina, offering me the position! I have been selected as the new Executive Director for Family Crisis Council of Rowan, Inc. (an organization focused on supporting, empowering, and advocating for victims and survivors of domestic violence, sexual assault, and human trafficking). How exciting! I am given the opportunity of a lifetime, to tap into my professional experience, academic training, creativity, leadership, and passion to benefit the community and make a positive difference in people's lives, while getting paid to do so! Who could ask for more?!?

Dreams really do come true, if you believe they will. You need only to have faith and believe that God will do for us that which we cannot do for ourselves, if only we are willing to believe in Him, put one foot in front of the other, and do the next right thing. God has shown Himself, His love, and His power over and over, time and time again.

I can honestly say that we are happier than we have ever been before, and I know it's not because of anything we did to deserve it. All we have done is remained sober, through all the difficulties, by God's grace, tried to help others, and maintained our membership in the 'No Matter What' Club. No matter what, we will not relinquish our sobriety, as our sobriety and our serenity are non-negotiable!

Kenneth and I are truly living our best lives, and it gets better every day. We are thriving as a true power couple, not only in our personal lives but also in our shared mission to make a difference through our international, virtual coaching and consulting business, *Consider it Done 20/20*. Our journey of recovery has only strengthened our bond, fueling our passion to help others navigate their own goals and challenges. We've combined our personal experiences, professional skills, and unwavering faith to create a platform where individuals can find the guidance and support they need to achieve their personal and professional goals.

Together, we're committed to empowering others to uncover their true purpose and live fulfilling lives. Whether it's overcoming obstacles, setting and achieving goals, or realizing their deepest desires, we are here to guide them every step of the way. Through *Consider it Done 20/20*, a life of sobriety, and a deep faith in God, we are living our best lives and helping others do the same.

Chapter 10 – Can't Wait to See What's Next

As I reflect on the past 21 years of continuous sobriety, I can't help but marvel at the transformative power of God's grace. Each year, each milestone, and each moment of victory over the darkness of addiction has been a testament to the gifts of God in my life. These gifts, though not always wrapped in the packages I expected, have been constant reminders of His love, mercy, and unyielding faithfulness. They've come in the form of wisdom gained through struggle, strength built through surrender, and the profound peace that comes from trusting in His plan.

Along with my sobriety, some of the greatest gifts God has given me is a marriage rooted in love, trust, and shared faith, loving parents, and amazing children. After years of living through drama, trauma, heartbreak, and despair, finding a partner in Kenneth who could walk this journey with me has been nothing short of miraculous. Together, we've experienced the beauty of a relationship where each of us is committed to our own personal growth, our marriage, our shared journey of faith, and a meaningful familial relationship. Our love story is a testament to the power of redemption and the joy that comes from a union blessed by God.

Through these years of sobriety and this happy marriage, I have come to realize that hindsight, when coupled with faith and obedience to God, can unlock a powerful vision for the future. This is what I call *20/20 Vision*—the ability to clearly see the lessons of the past and use them as a guide for what lies ahead. It is about turning hindsight into foresight, allowing the wisdom gained from past experiences to inform and shape the decisions we make today.

But unlocking this vision is not just about looking back; it's also about looking within. It requires a deep understanding of our purpose and being able to articulate our *why*—the reasons we get up in the morning, the motivations that drive us to succeed, and the vision that propels us toward becoming the best versions of ourselves. Identifying your purpose is crucial because it serves as the anchor in the storm, the compass that guides your journey, and the fuel that keeps you moving forward even when the road gets tough.

Living a life of purpose, faith, and trust in God means making choices that align with your values and motives. It is about having pure intentions and good motives in everything you do, ensuring that your actions reflect the principles of love, kindness, and integrity. When your motives are pure, your intentions are good, and you walk in obedience to God, you open yourself up to a life of fulfillment and divine favor.

As I stand on the other side of 21 years of sobriety, and Kenneth stands on the other side of 18 years of recovery, I can see clearly now how every moment of struggle, every heartbreak, and every tear was leading me to this point. The journey was not easy, but it was worth it. Through it all, God has been faithful, and He has turned what seemed like insurmountable challenges into blessings beyond my wildest dreams.

Understanding your purpose and being able to articulate your why is not just an exercise in self-discovery—it is a spiritual practice. When you know why you were created and what you were created to do, you can walk confidently in your purpose, knowing that every step you take is ordered by God. This clarity of purpose gives you the strength to face challenges head-on, the courage to pursue your dreams with passion, and the resilience to keep going even when the road gets tough.

Your purpose is not just about what you do; it is about who you are. It is about the legacy you leave behind, the impact you have on others, and the ways in which you reflect God's love and grace in the world. When you live with purpose, every day becomes an opportunity to make a difference, to be a light in the darkness, and to contribute to the greater good.

But purpose alone is not enough. To truly unlock your *20/20 Vision*, you must couple your purpose with faith, trust, and obedience to God. Faith gives you the assurance that even when you cannot see the path ahead, God is leading you. Trust allows you to release your fears and anxieties, knowing that God is in control. And obedience to God ensures that you are walking in His will, aligning your actions with His plan for your life.

As I close this chapter, and indeed this book, I want to leave you with this: Unlocking your *20/20 Vision* is not a one-time event, but a lifelong journey. It's about continually seeking God's guidance, trusting His timing, and staying true to your purpose. It's about allowing the lessons of the past to inform your present and guide your future. And it's about living each day with intention, gratitude, and a deep sense of purpose.

May you, too, unlock your *20/20 Vision*. May you see clearly the gifts of God in your life, the purpose for which you were created, and the path that lies ahead. And may you walk confidently into your future, knowing that with God by your side, anything is possible.

As you journey forward, remember this: The best is yet to come. Keep your eyes fixed on God, your heart anchored in His love, and your spirit open to His leading. In doing so, you will unlock a life of purpose, joy, and fulfillment—a life that truly reflects the glory of God.

I can hardly wait to see what's next, as this is not the end, but only the beginning of the rest of my life, your life, our lives…

Made in the USA
Columbia, SC
15 February 2025

53808202R00028